TURKISH STEAM RAILWAYS

Mick Pope

AMBERLEY

First published 2019

Amberley Publishing
The Hill, Stroud
Gloucestershire, GL5 4EP

www.amberley-books.com

ISBN 978 1 4456 8782 7 (print)
ISBN 978 1 4456 8783 4 (ebook)

British Library Cataloguing in Publication Data.
A catalogue record for this book is available from the British Library.

Origination by Amberley Publishing.
Printed in the UK.

Introduction

Turkey straddles Europe and Asia and reflects this in the mix of cultures from both continents to be found there. The western and southern coastal areas are the most familiar to Western holidaymakers but the interior, Black Sea coast and east of the country are less visited. Here there are borders with Syria, Iran and Russia, with a link through Syria to Iraq. This book is not intended to be a historical or technical account of Turkey's railways but an attempt to capture the essence of the railways and the way they weave into the environment and the lives of the people who work on and use them.

As Western railway enthusiasts found less and less to attract them in Europe, they discovered that Turkey had steam locomotives aplenty, reflecting the fact that this was a country that had embraced Western industrialisation and modernisation ahead of most other Middle Eastern countries. The history of the companies building, owning or overseeing the railways of Turkey is complicated and I am going to avoid trying to explain this in a brief introduction. This, and the shifting alliances and conflicts Turkey had embraced, are also reflected in the variety of countries that built steam locomotives for the railways, many of which started under foreign ownership. Examples could be found from locomotive builders in Germany, Sweden, France, the United States and the United Kingdom. These varied from ancient specimens of Prussian State Railway design to modern ten-coupled designs built after the Second World War. Gradually over a period of years the Turkish railways have been nationalised as Turkiye Cumhuriyeti Devlet Demiryollari Isletmesi, which is conveniently shortened to TCDD!

Finding and photographing trains presented certain problems. Train services in this large country could be sparse and timekeeping notoriously unreliable. There is an apocryphal tale of the foreign tourist who, aware of the notorious timekeeping, remarked to a local as his expected train arrived that this was fortunate. The local replied that this was the previous day's train, 24 hours late! The roads, very often of dirt, are hazardous due to the eccentric driving habits of the locals! The author had personal experience of this in a bizarre incident. While tearing down a dirt road to the next photographic location, an overloaded truck carrying sugar beet was encountered. The truck hit a rut in the road and half a dozen of the vegetable roots in question spilled and bounced along the road like the proverbial 'Dambusters' bouncing bomb. One bounced off the roof and the other scored a direct hit on our radiator. Overheating soon became apparent but this was Turkey and so in the next town a friendly local directed us to his brother's garage, a shop front on the main street, where the offending radiator was removed, welded, pressure-tested and reinstalled while we drank sweet

Turkish tea in the cafe opposite – all done for the equivalent of £5! Stereotypically, Turks were seen as a cruel people but I have always found them kind and friendly, apart from the two dark-suited and sunglass-wearing security policemen who asked us to leave Zonguldak when there was industrial unrest there!

The other side of the coin was seen the day I was perched alone on top of a hill overlooking the Kars line in the barren east of the country. I spied a uniformed figure making its way slowly up the hill. I began to expect an interrogation and possible incarceration. On arrival the man grasped my hand, shook it and reached inside his coat. I expected a badge or even a gun but he produced an apple, thrust it into my hand, smiled, said something I did not understand, and plodded back down the hill!

Politics and security issues could also create problems reflecting Turkey's membership of NATO and the proximity to Russia and the unstable regimes to the south and east. Using a camera in certain areas could result in a warning or a visit to the local police station. However, if these problems could be endured, the landscape offered fantastic photographic opportunities.

Doorway to Turkish steam – a first glimpse of a German-built 'Kriegslok' through the old but sturdy doors of a station waiting room.

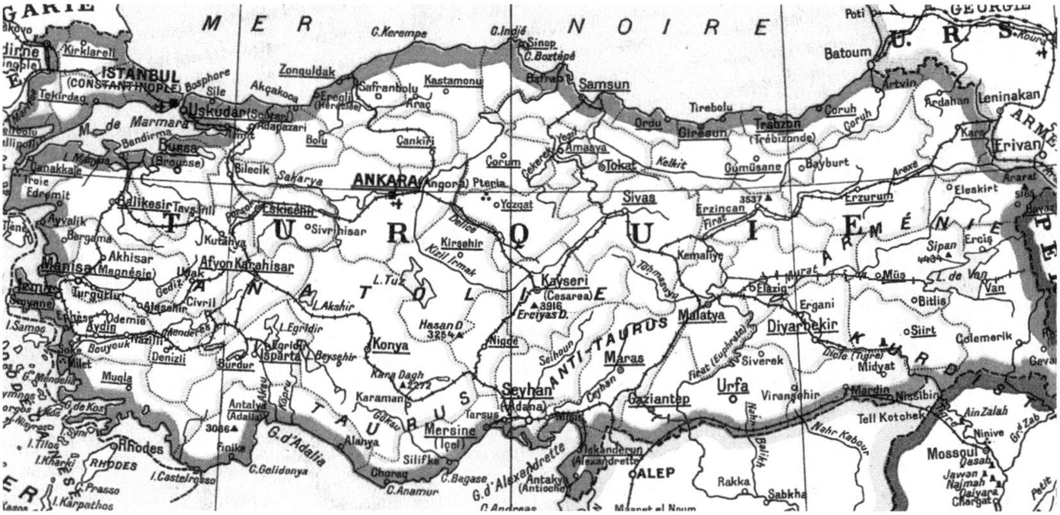

A 1950s French map of Turkey showing the major cities and rail routes with more recent lines in the east added. France was very involved in the development of Turkey's railways.

Western Turkey

Eastern and Western Turkey are linked by two routes. The southern route runs from Ulukişla to Afyon, an important junction, and on to Izmir via Manisa with a series of branches and minor lines en route. Izmir had a steam-hauled suburban service but sadly this was no longer in operation when I visited. To the north a line runs from Sivas via Kayseri, Irmak and Eskisehir and on to Istanbul. This line saw some diesel traction and steam-hauled traffic was sparse. North to south lines link Sivas and Ulukişla and Afyon to Eskisehir amid a network of minor and branch lines. A further east to west route runs to the south of the Afyon to Izmir via Manisa route. This runs through Aydin to Dinar and was lightly constructed, resulting in diesels not being permitted, and so steam remained in use, including on the branches to Denizli and Sutlac and those from Karakuyu, which feature in a chapter of their own. The line north of Izmir from Balikesir to the port of Bandirma, where a ferry ran to Istanbul, also saw steam action in later years. Lines out from Istanbul to Adapazari are electrified. Western Turkey saw the last regular steam workings.

Major steam depots in this area included Haydarpaşa in Istanbul, Halkapinar in Izmir, Eskisehir, Afyon, Usak, Kayseri and Konya with various local sub-sheds. A locomotive works repairing steam locomotives was sited at Halkapinar in Izmir.

Located near the ancient Greek city of Ephesus, Camlik is also the site of a railway museum. The loco pictured here was, however, still in revenue-earning service in 1988.

Just to the west of Dinar, this long freight with diesel and steam power on the front climbs through the barren mountains in October 1984.

Bringing up the rear of the long freight is another Kriegslok assisting the load up the gradient while the guard observes the photographers from his van.

The same train is seen again against the barren hillside with the steam locomotive still working hard.

A major feature of this route from Konya to Afyon is the climb to Bozdag, a wild and remote place. Unusually for Turkey, in spite of a long climb, pilot and banking locomotives were rarely used. Here a 46xxx class 2-8-2 approaches the summit with a passenger train in October 1985.

Near the same location a long freight hauled by a 561xx 2-10-0 climbs through the treeless landscape with its black smoke drifting over the dry grassland in October 1985.

The passenger train again. The snow fences give the clue that this must be a bleak environment in winter. October 1985.

A little further along the route, the passenger train runs on a ledge in the hillside. October 1985.

The locomotive hauling this freight over Bozdag has received some decorative attention.

This derelict, roofless building is the locomotive depot at Tavsanli, on the line to Izmir via Balikesir. Some steam locomotives still operated from the depot, mainly on shunting duties, although this 55xxx seemed to be out of service.

Here is the familiar sight of a Churchill, or Stanier 8F as British enthusiasts would know them. This one is No. 45168, which is now preserved at Izmit in Turkey. She was allegedly still available for use when this photo was taken at Tavsanli.

A possible choice from the remaining locomotives at Tavsanli for any shunting duties was this G10, No. 55030.

A line of spare 561xx 2-10-0s stands in the yard at Tavsanli. I believe they were called back into service not long after this photo was taken.

Here is another shot of No. 45168 in the shed yard at Tavsanli.

The active G10, No. 55041, waits its next duty at Tavsanli.

Cow and cart wait while a G10 shunts across their path.

In the last rays of the evening sun, a west-bound train hauled by a 57xxx 2-10-2 stops at a small country station in October 1985.

A veritable Turkish steam bath as a double-headed Kriegslok-hauled train passes a third example of that type stopped by a water column in October 1985.

The powerful outline of a standard 2-10-0 on freight duty, October 1985.

A lightweight 2-10-2 of the 57xxx class, No. 57018, stands at Kaklik to the west of Bozdag with a load of ballast wagons in October 1985.

A pair of Krieglsoks on a mixed train get the green flag from the linesman outside his hut in September 1984.

Some adjustments or repairs are required to the Kriegslok on this freight and the driver has edged his way along the running plate as the locomotive is stopped on the main line.

Kriegsloks did not have the monopoly of the freight traffic to the west of Konya, as this standard 2-10-0 illustrates.

The locomotives on this part of the system were generally kept in decent external condition and made an attractive sight in this part of Turkey, which was much greener than the eastern provinces.

This chap was determined to be photographed with one of his locomotives at Usak depot. This was one of the last to service steam locomotives, including those used on steam specials at the very end, and usable, and unusable, locomotives collected there.

A Kriegslok heads a freight, almost certainly sugar beet, across flat farmland west of Afyon.

In the gathering evening gloom a Krieglsok makes an impressive effort on an uphill section of the Afyon to Izmir line.

On the rear of the train in the previous picture is another Kriegslok, with the glow from the firebox illuminating the cab. It is 'banking' the train up the hill.

A station stop on the Afyon to Izmir section.

This is Camlik, near Ephesus. I must have been one of those rare tourists who chose to visit the station rather than the ancient ruins! Steam operated mainly on banking, ballast and shunting duties by this time, which is 1988.

Another view of the Kriegslok at Camlik with the signal cabin in view.

Locomotives based at Camlik had few facilities. This is what certain British locomotive depots would refer to as the 'coal hole'. A simple conveyor belt delivers coal from a stack into the locomotive's tender as it sits in a sunken stretch of track.

TCDD No. 46003 shunting at Adapazari station in October 1977. Located at the end of a branch off the electrified Istanbul to Ankara main line, shunting remained in the hands of steam. (Photo by Lou Johnson)

British-built 2-8-2 No. 46101 ready for departure at 17.30 from Manisa to Alesehir in October 1977. It was built by Robert Stephenson in 1929. (Photo by Lou Johnson)

A local sits in quiet contemplation as the NOHAB of Sweden-built 2-6-0 rests in a siding. This locomotive was a regular on the Manisa to Izmir service at the time.

Probably my favourite among the Turkish locomotives is the neatly proportioned 2-6-0 built by NOHAB.

No. 56547 with a mixed train on the line to Bandirma in September 1984. (Photo by Lou Johnson)

End of the line at the port of Bandirma. A 2-10-0 stands near the quayside with some modern coaches.

A final view of the typical motive power in western Turkey during the latter years of Turkish steam.

Dinar and the Branches to Burdur Isparta and Egridir

This area was much visited by enthusiasts as it was one of the last to retain steam power, had, by Turkish standards, a frequent and complex service, and the lines ran through scenic terrain. The sugar beet harvest season around October saw extra trains being used to carry the produce. It was particularly popular with German enthusiasts as the main motive power included eight- and ten-coupled locomotives of Prussian G8 and G10 designs dating from the 1920s plus the famous wartime German Class 52 Kriegsloks of 2-10-0 wheel arrangement. These latter locos were originally hired by Turkish Railways but this became a permanent arrangement. Also working on the system were the 57xxx class of lightweight 2-10-2s, which were also from German builders and of 1930s vintage. These locos combined the boilers of the larger 46xxx class of 4-8-0s with the chassis of the G10.

The branches diverged from the most southerly of the three lines connecting Afyon with Izmir at the junction station of Karakuyu. There were locomotive depots at Burdur and Egridir at the end of two of the branches but not at the Isparta terminus. Locomotives were also serviced at Dinar a little way along the main line from Karakuyu. The train services included through 'express' coaches to Izmir running in trains of usually two vehicles – surely some of the smallest and slowest such trains in the world! There was some tender-first working, particularly up the Isparta branch, where there was no turntable.

Popular places for photography were the steep climb at Keciborlu near Karakuyu, the junction for the Isparta branch at Gumusgun and a spectacular curved viaduct on the approach to Egridir with a large lake in the background. The latter named town was close to a Turkish Army training area and enthusiasts were often questioned by police if seen with cameras in the locality. Sadly the section to Egridir is now closed, although I believe the station buildings still survive.

A pre-First World War German-built G8 0-8-0 at Bozanonu.

The locomotive depot at Dinar with one of the 57xxx 2-10-2s in residence in October 1988.

Another shot of the same locomotive in October 1988.

No. 57009, built by Henschel of Germany in 1933, was a regular performer out of Dinar, both on the Isparta branch and to the west on the main line. Here she stands outside the depot at Dinar in light steam in October 1988.

Here is a view of the servicing area at Dinar with a steam crane for coaling, a water tower and a water column. A 565xx Kriegslok is being watered here in October 1988.

A closer look at the coaling crane with 2-10-2 No. 57009 awaiting its turn in October 1988.

A 55xxx class 0-10-0 built to a Prussian design in the 1920s, seen here outside Dinar locomotive depot.

A final view of the shed with a variety of locomotives at rest in October 1988.

Karakuyu is the junction on the main line to Izmir where diesel-hauled trains and railcars on the main line connected with the steam-hauled trains on the branch lines to Burdur, Isparta and Egridir. The station was a little way from the actual village of the same name. An unusual 'balloon' loop allowed trains from Afyon and Dinar to enter the branch system without the need to reverse. Here, a train hauled by a DE18 class waits in the platform while a 565xx Kriegslok awaits its next duty in the sidings. The steam-era infrastructure is very obvious here in October 1988!

Latterly the Kriegsloks were increasingly used on the system, replacing older German designs. Here, one waits in Karakuyu station with a 'mixed' train.

Passengers cross the tracks in front of a Kriegslok shunting wagons to be loaded with sugar beet in October 1988.

The Kriegslok backs its wagons into the loading dock, where local farmers wait with loads of sugar beet on their trucks and trailers in October 1988.

On another occasion, a Prussian-designed G10 0-8-0, No. 55043, pulls its train through Karakuyu station bound for Dinar in October 1985.

A G8 shunting a mixed assortment of wagons.

A crew member checks around the motion of his locomotive at Karakuyu. The coach in the background is probably part of the 'express' service to Istanbul, usually just a couple of coaches.

The crew of a Kriegslok mounts its steed and prepares to depart in October 1988.

A group of station staff enjoys a chat while the Kriegslok simmers away in the loop.

The first of a sequence of photos taken on the day an enthusiasts' special toured the Burdur system. Here a Kriegslok waits with a scheduled service in Karakuyu station.

The enthusiasts' special arrives at Karakuyu behind another Kriegslok in October 1985. Generally locomotives in this area of Turkey were kept in reasonable external condition.

A third loco joins the line-up at Karakuyu. This is a G8, which was participating in a railtour and replacing the larger locomotive, hence its well-turned-out appearance. October 1985.

The G8 scheduled for the railtour was earlier waiting near the water crane. In the foreground a local woman picks coal from the ashes cleaned from a locomotive's ash pan. This was something I was familiar with from India, but I was surprised to see it occurring in a relatively developed country.

The G8 takes the special out of Karakuyu.

Beyond Karakuyu the line crosses a wide, flat plain and, for the sake of continuity, here is the enthusiasts' special again, now heading for the next junction at Gumusgun in October 1985.

After the stretch across the flat plain, trains face a stiff climb up to Keciborlu, and here the fireman of the special has clearly been at work filling the firebox for the effort in October 1985.

Here a combination of G8 No. 44055 and G10 No. 55034 is pulling a mixed train consisting of two passenger vehicles and a following rake of assorted freight wagons, taking the climb to Keciborlu in September 1984.

A long freight train, with the locomotives unusually coupled tender to tender, plods up the gradient towards Keciborlu.

Unseen in the previous picture, at the rear of the train was a third locomotive acting as a 'banker' to push the long train up the steep gradient. Here it has dropped off and will coast back down the hill.

Another class of locomotive on the gradient, in this case a Kriegslok, passes a gang of permanent way workers.

A Kriegslok attacks the gradient with a passenger train, a portent of things to come as the class gradually took over from the older types.

A G8-hauled regular service train crosses the rather bleak plain after leaving Karakuyu.

Introducing the other locomotive class that worked the Burdur branches – the lightweight 2-10-2s in the 57xxx number series. Here No. 57009 is working the two 'express' through coaches to and from Istanbul and is standing at Gumusgun.

A G8 trundles tender-first along the Isparta branch with its two-coach express.

Dwarfed by the spectacular Turkish scenery, a 57xxx 2-10-2 works a train from Isparta to the junction.

G8 No. 44017 has lost some of her shine after starring in the enthusiasts' tour and has now reverted back to her normal appearance alongside a Prussian sister at Gumusgun.

A pair of German-built locomotives departing from Gumusgun.

G8 No. 44017 has arrived at Gumusgun and the crew has spotted a problem with the valve gear.

Further examination of the G8 by a blue-coated official while the driver of the G10 seems disinterested in the problem.

As with most problems with steam-age technology in Turkey, there was little that could not be solved by the use of a large hammer and a spanner!

A second train has arrived at Gumusgun, a busy location in the October sugar beet season.

The two trains have combined and will leave the station as a 'double-header'.

New and old forms of transport on the Burdur system. Sugar beet arrived at transhipment points behind tractors, trucks, horses and mules.

This is the branch to Burdur and the lake of that name is visible in the background.

The locomotive yard at Burdur terminus with a G8 in residence and the tender of a Kriegslok just visible behind it.

The old chap in the foreground was determined to be photographed in front of this equally vintage machine at Burdur!

The enthusiasts' special seen in earlier shots crosses a viaduct as it descends into Egridir.

Another view of the end of the line, sadly no longer a possibility. The station building, with its small 'train shed', is particularly attractive.

A mixed train climbs out of Egridir with the lake of that name in the background.

The Zonguldak to Irmak Route

The line from Zonguldak on the Black Sea runs southwards to join the main west to east route through the central spine of Turkey at Irmak. There are major industrial complexes in the Zonguldak area including ports, steelworks and coal mines. Sadly at the time of my visit there had been suspected terrorist activity and industrial unrest, and so access to much of the areas of interest in the coastal area was prohibited. Steam activity on the main line varied with the availability of diesels and few trains were consistently steam. Those that ran did so behind the Skyliner 2-10-0s, so called because of the smooth casing covering pipework along the boiler top. These locomotives were built by Vulcan Ironworks in the United States in the late 1940s. At some points on the line double-heading or banking by a second locomotive was required. Scenery varied from flat valley bottoms to steep climbs through rocky hills. Locomotive depots at Catalagzi, Cankiri and Karabuk served the line.

The main motive power on this line comes from the big American-built 2-10-0s known to enthusiasts as 'Skyliners'. The nickname is explained by the smooth casing over the pipe work along the boiler top. Out on the main line an unusually tender-to-tender-coupled pair works southwards through the sunburnt grassland towards Cankiri and Irmak in September 1984.

More local power and shunting was in the hands of the S200 'Middle East' 2-8-2s built for the United States Army Transportation Corps. Here No. 46244 runs light to its next duty with the shunter riding on the buffer beam in September 1984.

The 'Middle East' 2-8-2 shunts the yard at Catalagzi, with the driver watching the photographer's activities with interest, in September 1984.

Another 'Middle East' stands outside the locomotive depot at Catalagzi in September 1984.

Another US product, Skyliner No. 56304, outside the shed at Catalagzi in September 1984.

A detailed view of a Skyliner cab and below it the steam injector gear, seen in September 1984.

The shed at Catalagzi was small by Western standards and considering the size of the locomotives it housed. Here, another Skyliner rests, awaiting a call to duty in September 1984.

Older types of locomotives could often be found around depots in Turkey, abandoned in sidings for long spells. Here is a 1912-built 2-6-0, No. 34008, from Borsig of Berlin, seen quietly rusting away without its tender at Catalagzi in September 1984.

A 'little brother' to the US-built 'Middle East 2-8-2s, the USATC S160 2-8-0 was a locomotive type found in many countries, including such far-flung places as India and China, after the Second World War, for which they mainly owe their existence. By the 1980s they were becoming worn out and many examples such as this example, slowly rusting away at Catalagzi in September 1984, had been set aside.

Completing a trio of North American-built locomotives at Catalagzi in September 1984 is this Skyliner, No. 56304.

A view from inside the locomotive depot at Catalagzi in September 1984 with a 'Middle East' parked outside.

Out on the line between Zongulzac and Cankiri, a Skyliner pounds along on one of the flatter sections in September 1984.

Not quite sure why there is this unusual configuration of tender-to-tender-coupled locos in September 1984 but the second Skyliner seems not to be working very hard and may have a problem; it may be on its way to the works for repair.

The leading Skyliner looks not long through the 'shops' after overhaul in September 1984.

The train begins a climb with signs of life from the second locomotive in September 1984.

Another view of the same train, September 1984. (Photo by Lou Johnson)

The line had flat stretches in river valleys, mostly dry at this time of the year – September 1984.

Seemingly passing through a fairly flat landscape between Catalagzi and Cankiri in September 1984 is another Skyliner-hauled freight. However, a gradient cannot be far away as the consist was completed by another of the class for 'banking' on the next climb. Or perhaps we should use the American term of a 'helper' locomotive!

The second Skyliner pushes at the rear of the train. September 1984.

A little further on, the gradient begins to get steeper. September 1984. (Photo by Lou Johnson)

The rear of the train passes the photographer with the Skyliner still filling the sky with black smoke. September 1984.

With the long train visible rounding the curve ahead but the locomotive already out of sight, the banking locomotive digs in to the climb. September 1984.

Another freight traverses the treeless grassland through which sections of the line passed. September 1984.

Speeding along a flatter stretch, a Skyliner-hauled train heads towards Cankiri. September 1984.

A long shot of the train in typical Turkish countryside of rolling bare hills and green valleys dotted with cypress trees. September 1984.

Cankiri is an intermediate point on the line where engines could be changed and there was a locomotive depot. Here, two Skyliners stand in the station in September 1984.

Looking as though it has fairly recently been through the shops at Sivas Works is Skyliner No. 56341, standing in the station area at Cankiri in September 1984.

The late sun glints off the side of this Skyliner as it heads for the depot in September 1984.

This is what British railwaymen and enthusiasts would sometimes call a 'dido' – a short taxi service between a station and a locomotive depot for the benefit of footplate staff. The motive power is somewhat excessive for the size of the train, seen in September 1984.

Another view of the 'dido' standing in the station yard. September 1984.

Skyliner No. 56338 south of Cankiri, working hard on the section to Irmak and the junction with the rest of the railway system. (Photo by Lou Johnson)

A British locomotive among a host of American ones! Stanier 8F No. 45153 is seen shunting at Cankiri in June 1980. (Photo by Lou Johnson)

Turkish Railways (TCDD) 2-8-0 No. 45161 is seen at Irmak depot in July 1968. Built in the UK by North British in 1941 for the War Department using the tried and tested LMS 8F design, this locomotive was originally numbered in the WD lists as 362, and later as 522. At the end of the war this locomotive and nineteen other 8Fs worked in Turkey, where they were nicknamed 'Churchills'. (Photo by Lou Johnson)

Central and Eastern Turkey

The railway routes in the east of Turkey were built comparatively late in the day, some not until the 1960s. They connect the country with Russia, Iran, Iraq and Syria. The east is much less populated than the west and the train service was quite sparse, although cities such as Erzurum actually had what passed as a suburban service. This was, and still is, a politically sensitive region and one had to be careful when taking photographs. The landscape is often desolate but spectacular. For many years the locomotives working in the eastern area were oil-fired, not surprising given the proximity to oil-producing states, but latterly more coal-fired locomotives found their way there.

The locomotive stock in the east was not very diverse and most trains were worked by the standard 56xxx 2-10-0s. The exception was the line from Sivas to Samsun and its branches, and this has its own place in this book. Sadly my travels did not take me to the lines to the south-east of the country and so the photos are confined to the line to Kars and the Russian border.

A local woman takes a shortcut through the yard at Kayseri with the yard pilot, an S160 2-8-0.

A work-stained ex-USATC S160 acts as yard pilot at Kayseri.

Another view of an S160 at Kayseri.

An interest in steam locomotives is not a recognised hobby in Turkey and so this young lad is somewhat bemused by the interest the photographer is showing.

A military companion for the S160, this 'Middle East' 2-8-2 is seen enveloped in its own steam. Built on a 'lend-lease' basis for the British War Department by US manufacturers in 1942–43, a batch was sold to Turkish Railways after the end of the Second World War. This example is also shunting at Kayseri.

Completing a trio of US-built shunters at Kayseri is this Skyliner, reduced to menial tasks.

These 2-8-2s, built in Germany by Henschel in 1937, were perhaps the only class that could be described as passenger engines. They were originally used on the Istanbul to Ankara main line until replaced by more modern motive power and seemed well liked at their home depot of Konya, where they were kept in good condition. This one is seen at Kayseri on a train for Konya in September 1984.

The clean appearance and brass boiler bands suggest this locomotive was a 'pet' as far as its crew was concerned!

It's all action as staff replenish the water supply of the big locomotive while locals look on. September 1984.

It looks as though the crew are filling the firebox with coal and getting ready for departure in September 1984 as two young boys admire the big beast – Turkish trainspotters?

The 'standard' 2-10-0s in the 56xxx and 561xx series have a very similar profile to the 2-8-2s. This example is at Kayseri in September 1984.

Henschel 2-8-2 No. 46056 heading a mixed train towards Konya in September 1984. (Photo by Lou Johnson)

Out to the east, a 2-10-0-hauled mixed train heads towards Erzincan in October 1985, through the desolate but breathtaking scenery typical of this part of Turkey.

There is not a steam locomotive at the head of this train in October 1985 but steam still plays a part. Diesel locomotives at this time could not heat steam-heated carriages and so boiler vans were employed, and here an example in corporate livery is coupled behind the locomotive.

In rather inclement weather in October 1985 a standard 2-10-0 heads a two-coach passenger train past an unimpressed herd of goats.

The same train speeds along a level stretch of track. The locomotive looks in good condition and bears signs of having had white-painted buffers.

The large locomotive is toy-like in the sweeping, bare landscape of eastern Turkey.

A 2-10-0 leading a mixed train heads off into the east towards Kars and the distant mountains.

In the far south of this area, 2-6-0 No. 34062 prepares for a mixed train to Karamanmaras at Kopruagzi in October 1977. The locomotive was built by Henschel in Germany in 1933. (Photo Lou Johnson)

The locomotive depot at Elazig on the route to Iran via Lake Van. 'Middle East' class 2-8-2s predominate. (Photo by Lou Johnson)

Sivas to Samsun and the Carsamba Branch

This is another individual line where a specific class of locomotives predominated. Samsun is one of Turkey's Black Sea ports and the railway linked it to the main west to east line at Sivas, where major railway repair and maintenance workshops are located. The line was built as late as 1932 as the state railway system gradually extended eastwards. However, there had been much earlier plans, in 1873, to build a railway along the coast from Samsun westwards to Bafra and eastwards to Carsamba to serve the local tobacco industry. This project did not get underway until 1924 and the line was built to a 750 mm gauge. Only the section from Samsun to Carsamba was completed. This line was closed in 1971 but somewhat surprisingly was rebuilt to standard gauge and reopened in 1980 with a further short branch to an industrial complex at Azot from a junction just outside Samsun. The Carsamba line runs along the coast for the first part of its route before heading inland, with stops at small towns and villages en route, and arriving at its terminus. The last stretch is along the main street, past shops, and ends abruptly in buffer stops.

The main line to Sivas runs through some dramatic mountainous scenery and some trains had to be double-headed.

Traffic on the main line and branch lines prior to dieselisation was handled almost exclusively by 45xxx 2-8-0s.

Today there are plans to rebuild sections of the main line, diverting it to arrive in Samsun via Carsamba, thus avoiding some of the steeper gradients.

A view across the harbour at Samsun with a 45xxx 2-8-0 running along lines near to the terminus.

An elevated view of the busy harbour at Samsun in 1984.

A loco shunts at an industrial site in Samsun in 1984 with a loading facility in the background, probably for coal or scrap, which are important commodities in the area.

Early mornings were busy at Samsun station with trains departing to Carsamba, Sivas and the industrial estate at Azot. Here, the 45xxx 2-8-0s are assembling their trains.

A crew member from No. 45017 gets in the picture as his loco's safety valve lifts.

Sidelined at Samsun and gradually being taken over by vegetation is this 2-6-2 tank built by Maffei of Munich in 1911. They were originally built as well tanks but were rebuilt with side tanks. This loco may have been allocated here to work the branch lines or possibly just to shunt in the yard, but by this date the 45xxx 2-8-0s had a monopoly of all duties.

Heading away from Samsun is this lightweight mixed train.

With the Black Sea off to the right, the Carsamba train, quite lengthy for a branch line, heads eastwards towards its destination.

A neat intermediate station on the branch with a platform rather too short for the length of the train!

At another station en route to Carsamba the loco crew chats with station staff waiting to give them the right of way.

Just alongside the Carsamba branch was the colliery at Suluova, which had a 600 mm narrow gauge line. The two locos, built by Henschel and Krauss, were preserved in a somewhat perfunctory manner.

A matching pair of officials to go with the pair of preserved locomotives!

Two forms of Turkish transport in one photo!

The train has arrived at Carsamba and the locomotive is uncoupled to run round its train for the return journey.

Looking in the opposite direction at the absolute end of the line. There cannot be many places where the railway terminates in the centre of the main street.

A neatly turned out 45xxx 2-8-0 on passenger duty between Samsun and Amasya.

In contrast, a freight passes through some of the more dramatic scenery. This class of locomotive seemed happy handling both passenger and freight traffic.

The early morning sun glints off the 2-8-0 as it progresses northwards from Samsun.

In a steep-sided gorge a passenger train pops in and out of tunnels as it passes through a rocky ridge between Samsun and Sivas.

The train has a tethered spectator!

A Samsun to Sivas service stops at an intermediate station and the crew checks over the valve gear.

Time to top up the tender tank.

The fireman takes the opportunity to shovel coal, or should that be coal dust, forward ready for the next stretch of the line. Meanwhile, passengers take the opportunity to stretch their legs on the platform.

A seemingly crowded passenger service climbs through higher, more barren countryside en route to Sivas.

A pair of 45xxx 2-8-0s working hard on a freight between Samsun and Sivas.

Another intermediate stop at a smaller station, without the luxury of a proper platform.

The fireman has filled the firebox with coal and is ready for departure.

Workers at Sivas Locomotive Works pass the plinthed 'gate guard', an 0-6-0 built by Hanomag in 1872.

A line-up of 2-8-0s at Sivas depot.

A rather dusty and seemingly work-stained 45xxx 2-8-0 in the yard at Sivas.

Turkey only built two locomotives on its own soil and this is one of them. Constructed mostly from spare parts in 1961 to the standard Henschel 2-10-0 design of 1937, No. 56202 is named *Bozkurt*, which translates as 'Grey Wolf'. Here she is out of use at Sivas Locomotive Works in 1985.

Another image of Turkish-built locomotive No. 56202 *Bozkurt* of 1937.

A familiar sight to British enthusiasts, Stanier 8F 2-8-0s were used overseas by the British military in the Middle East. Twenty-five were sold to Turkish Railways but seven were lost at sea en route. Two more were subsequently delivered. Known locally as 'Churchills', they received some modifications. This pair, Nos 45166 and 45155, were out of use at Sivas Works in 1984. The former is now preserved in Israel.

Another view of the British locos at Sivas. The barrel-like objects on the running plate are air reservoirs for the brake system.

This 2-6-0, No. 34057, was built by NOHAB of Sweden in 1930. Out of use, she was later scrapped. Just behind this loco is a Kreigslok that appears to have suffered some accidental damage while separated from its tender.

A scene captured near Sivas with a diesel-piloted 56xxx 2-10-0 on a freight service. It was normal practice in Turkey for diesels to be coupled in front of steam locos, unlike in many other countries where the opposite was the norm.